Foundation Curriculum
Copyright © 2014
Written by Linda D. Washington
Illustrated by Rebeca Flott
Edited by Joyce S. Pace and Rita K. Jeffries

STORY BOOK LESSON 1
"CREATION"

Jesus told us to pray and say,
"Our Father, in Heaven
We pray that Your name will always be kept holy!"

Listen closely to our story to find out why Jesus told us to pray like this!

Did you know that God is your heavenly Father?

Your heavenly Father lives in heaven. Heavenly Father is holy! Holy means that He is perfect. Heavenly Father does everything right, and there is no one greater than Him!

And guess who Heavenly Father loves?
You!

Your heavenly Father is a Spirit.
You cannot see Him with your eyes.

He does not have a body with skin or flesh and bones like you and me.

Touch the flesh on your arm, and feel the bone in your arm. Do you think heavenly Father has a flesh and bone body?

No, because Father is a Spirit.

Your Father is good and always tells the truth.
Since Father always tells the truth,
do you think you can trust Him?

Yes, you can trust your heavenly Father!

You can pray and talk to Him.

You can tell Him everything!

Do you know why God, your Father, loves you
so much?

Father loves you because God is Love!

Did you know that when your heavenly Father speaks, His Word creates life?

God's Word makes things come alive!
Every Word that God says is true and must happen!
Your heavenly Father spoke Words and created the sky and the earth and everything in them in six days.
And guess who He did it for?

For You!

Listen to what He did!

On Day 1,

God created the sky and earth.

The earth did not have any shape. The earth was empty and had deep dark waters. The Spirit of God, your heavenly Father moved over the water. And He spoke and said, "Let there be light!"

What do you think happened when Father spoke?

When Father said, "let there be light," there was light! God called the light day. And the darkness He called night. Father knew that you would need light to see. Father loves you! Let's thank Him and clap for Him! Thank you Father!

We are clapping for you! You're the best!

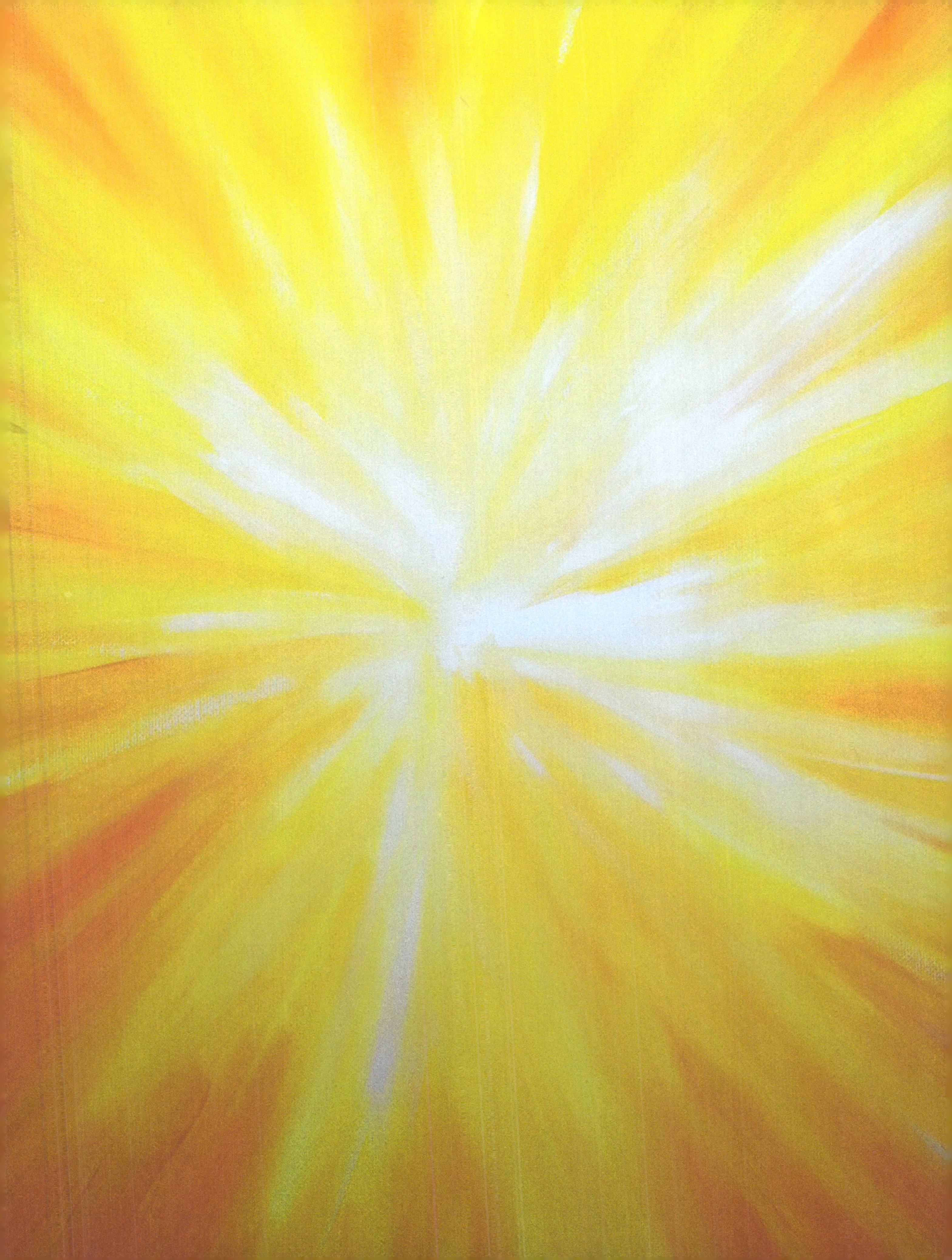

He kept thinking about you, so on
Day 2,
Father spoke to the deep dark waters and told them to be a firmament.

Firmament means to spread out, and for the waters to divide, with some above and some beneath. Do you think the waters obeyed Him? They sure did! And Father called the firmament above Sky or Heaven.

So far God has made two things, light for you to see, and a beautiful sky. What do you think is the next thing Father spoke to make for you?

Let's see.

On Day 3,

He said, "Let the water under the sky be gathered together so that the dry land may appear."

And the waters below the sky obeyed what Father said! And Father named the dry land earth. And the waters He called seas.

Father kept thinking about you and knew that you would need something to eat. So He spoke and told the earth to grow vegetables, and plants with seeds, and every kind of fruit tree with the seed in it. He made everything so that it would grow again from the seed in it.

Your Father is very good and He loves you! He made the earth for you to live on and food for you to eat. He keeps thinking about you. Let's Thank Him! Thank you Father!

On Day 4,

Father said, "Let there be lights in the sky. These lights will separate the days from the nights!"

And it obeyed Him! And God made two great lights. Do you know the name of the light He made for the day?

God made the sun to give you light for the day. Do you know the name of the lights He made to light the sky at night?

God made the moon and the stars for you to see at night.

On Day 5,

Father said, "Let the water be filled with many living things. And let there be birds to fly in the air over the earth!"

And God made all the water animals.
And He made birds to fly in the air over the earth.
He made the water animals and birds to have their
seed inside them so they could have babies.
And everything happened just the way Father said!

On Day 6,

Father said, "let the earth produce many kinds of living things!"

And God made animals such as cattle, goats, dogs, cats, horses, cows and every creeping thing that is on the earth.

Father looked at everything He had made, and guess what He saw?

Father saw everything that He had made was good! Father had worked to make the earth ready.

Do you know who Father made the earth ready for?

For His children!

Father had made the earth ready for all His children!

It was time to make a man and woman. Father said let us make man and woman to look like us and to be like us! And let them rule over fish, birds, animals, crawling things, and the whole earth! God made His children! And He blessed them. God put a good seed inside of the first man. And every person was born from the seed of the first man.

Who do you think Father made His children to be like?

He made you and all His children to be like Him!

He made you to speak words that give life.

Father made you to love Him and all people, just like He loves you!

Do you think God was finished with His work? Yes, your Father was finished with all of His work! What do you think Father did on the seventh day? He rested! He blessed the seventh day and made it holy and special.

Father had made His children!

Can you see that Father loves you every day by the things He has done? This is why you should pray to Father in heaven everyday because He loves you. You can pray and tell Him with your words that He is holy and sacred. You can pray to Him from your heart and He will hear you. You can praise and rave about your good Father! You can brag and boast about Father right now! You can lift up your hands or just tell Him with your own words, like this:

"Thank you for loving me!
You are Awesome Father!
I am raising my hands up to You!
Ya-Hoo Father! I am blowing kisses to You!
Glory to your name!
I thank you from my heart!
I love you Father!"

The Purpose of the Foundation Curriculum

To firmly establish God's truth in each child's heart early in life so they will understand and know God's love and choose to live fully in the victory that Jesus Christ has already won.

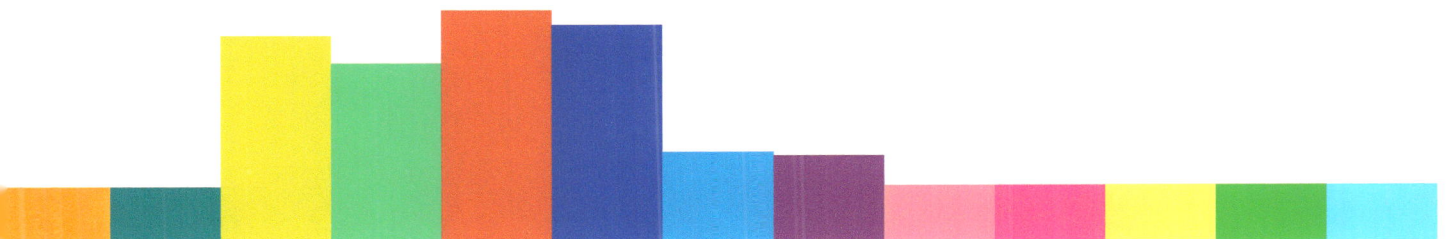

The Goals

To show God's children his love, their true identity as children of God, their authority and power in Christ Jesus, their helper Holy Spirit, and how to pray to their Father in heaven.

CREATION

Story Book Lesson 1

The Objectives to understand from "Creation" are:

1. God is LOVE.

2. God is your heavenly Father.

3. Father loves you!

4. Heavenly Father is Holy and Spirit. (Holy Spirit)

5. You were made in God's image, a spirit who loves.

6. All people were born from the seed inside the first man, Adam.

7. Father made all things by His Word.

8. Father will talk with you in prayer.

9. You can thank and praise Father for loving you first.

P.A.C.E.

Products and Activities
for Christian Education

For Free Follow-Up Activities to Reinforce This Story Book Lesson Please Visit
www.ABC-Jesus.com

Biblical quotes were from different versions of the holy Bible.